Pitshou Moleka

Glossary of Technical Words in the Field of Innovation

Pitshou Moleka

Glossary of Technical Words in the Field of Innovation

ScienciaScripts

Imprint

Cover image: www.ingimage.com

This book is a translation from the original published under ISBN 978-620-6-72130-7.

Publisher:
Sciencia Scripts
is a trademark of
Dodo Books Indian Ocean Ltd. and OmniScriptum S.R.L publishing group

120 High Road, East Finchley, London, N2 9ED, United Kingdom
Str. Armeneasca 28/1, office 1, Chisinau MD-2012, Republic of Moldova, Europe
Printed at: see last page
ISBN: 978-620-8-26366-9

PITSHOU MOLEKA, PhD

LEXICON OF TECHNICAL WORDS IN THE FIELD OF INNOVATION

INTRODUCTION

Innovationology is a fast-growing field that takes an in-depth look at the processes, practices and concepts associated with innovation in all its forms. Based on the pioneering work of researcher Pitshou Moleka, this dynamic glossary takes you to the heart of the main theories, methodologies and issues shaping contemporary innovation. A genuine reference tool for researchers and practitioners, this glossary contains over a hundred specialised terms, covering a wide spectrum from methodological approaches to innovative economic models, organisational dynamics and societal issues. Each definition is accompanied by detailed explanations and sometimes concrete examples to help you grasp the richness and complexity of innovation. This glossary opens the door to an in-depth understanding of innovation ecosystems on a global scale. Let us guide you on an exciting exploration of the new frontiers of innovation!

Automatic adaptation: The ability of an intelligent system to adjust dynamically to changes in context or environment, based on machine learning and self-optimisation.

Organisational agility: The ability of an organisation to adapt quickly and effectively to changes in its environment, by encouraging flexibility and experimentation.

Sustainable agriculture: Agricultural practices that preserve the environment, ensure long-term food security and social well-being.

Climate-smart agriculture: An agricultural approach that aims to increase productivity and resilience in the face of climate change.

Agroecology: An integrated approach that applies ecological concepts and principles to the design and management of sustainable food systems.

Angels: Angels are individual investors who provide financial support to start-ups in exchange for a stake in the company. They also contribute their expertise and networks to help entrepreneurs succeed.

Anticipation: Developed by futurists such as Bertrand de Jouvenel, anticipation involves systematically exploring possible futures. Example: Long-term scenarios developed by the Stockholm Resilience Centre.

Anthropology of innovation: An emerging field of anthropology which studies the social, cultural and organisational processes involved in innovation, in order to better understand the dynamics of the creation, adoption and dissemination of innovations.

Agile learning: An approach to learning and skills development, conceptualised by training specialists, that encourages agility, iteration and the continuous adaptation of employees.

Algorithmic art: A form of digital art in which works are conceived and generated using computer algorithms, exploring the creative potential of artificial intelligence. Frieder Nake, a painter and mathematician, was a pioneer of this computer-generated art. His works explore the interactions between mathematics, computer science and aesthetics, challenging traditional notions of creativity and authorship.

Badges and micro-certifications: These are digital certificates issued to recognise specific skills, often acquired informally or as part of online training. They enable more granular recognition of learning.

Well-being at work: A concept developed by human capital specialists, representing the quality of life and the work environment that promotes employee fulfilment and performance.

Bio-inspiration or **biomimicry**: An approach to innovation that draws inspiration from the systems, processes and patterns found in nature to design sustainable and efficient solutions. Architect Mick Pearce designed the Eastgate shopping centre in Harare, Zimbabwe, using the thermoregulation of termite mounds as inspiration.

Bionanotechnology: An emerging field combining the principles of biology and nanotechnology, aimed at developing systems and materials with innovative properties inspired by living organisms.

Bionics: Discipline that draws inspiration from biological forms, structures and processes to design innovative objects, machines or systems.

Blockchain: Decentralised, secure and transparent information storage and transmission technology that creates tamper-proof digital registers and guarantees the traceability of transactions. The Kickstarter crowdfunding platform uses blockchain to secure transactions between creators and contributors.

Botswana Prosperity Index: An index developed by Pitshou Moleka to measure sustainable, inclusive and cultural prosperity in Botswana.

Burn-out: Concept developed by the psychoanalyst Herbert Freudenberger, referring to a state of physical, emotional and mental exhaustion resulting from chronic professional stress.

Green capitalism: Proposed transformation of the capitalist system towards a more environmentally-friendly economy, theorised by economists such as Paul Ekins. Example: "Green capitalism" initiatives of the International Monetary Fund.

Researcher-Entrepreneur: This concept, developed by experts at the Eudoxia Research Center in India, refers to a person who is able to combine the skills and expertise of a researcher and an entrepreneur, combining scientific rigour with entrepreneurial creativity to develop innovative solutions based on scientific research. For example, the biotechnology company Moderna was founded by academic researchers who were able to transform their discoveries into breakthrough innovations.

Intelligent robotic surgery (Intuitive Surgical): Intelligent robotic surgery uses surgical robots piloted by a surgeon, with the integration of artificial intelligence. This enables greater precision, better visualisation and faster recovery for patients.

Intuitive Surgical has developed the Da Vinci surgical robot, which is used in a wide range of minimally invasive procedures.

Flipped classroom: The flipped classroom is a teaching model in which learners study theoretical content beforehand, then use class time for practical activities, discussions and problem-solving, with the teacher's guidance.

Co-construction of public policies: Policy development in close collaboration with citizens and users.

Co-creation: A concept promoted by specialists in open innovation, this collaborative process between different stakeholders makes it possible to design and develop innovative solutions, making the most of their ideas, needs and feedback. LEGO has launched co-creation platforms with its users to develop new play sets.

Co-evolution: Innovation process in which innovations and their environment co-evolve dynamically, each influencing the other. For example, the emergence of digital technologies has led to the co-evolution of companies' business models to adapt to these new opportunities.

21st-century skills and soft skills: 21st-century skills encompass the soft skills and know-how essential for success in a rapidly changing world: critical thinking, creativity, communication, collaboration, digital literacy, independent learning, etc. These "soft skills" are increasingly valued by employers.

Cross-disciplinary skills: A concept developed by training experts to designate generic skills and aptitudes (communication, problem-solving, creativity, etc.) that can be transferred to different professional contexts.

Human-centred design: A design methodology that places the needs, capabilities and aspirations of users at the heart of the innovation process. Aims to develop solutions that are adapted to and accepted by end users.

Experience-oriented design: Design approach focused on creating enriching and meaningful user experiences. Focuses on user interaction, emotion and engagement.

Distributed design: Collaborative design process involving multiple interconnected players on a local or global scale. Promotes open innovation and co-creation through digital networks.

Function-oriented design: Innovation methodology centred on defining the functions expected of a product or system, rather than its technical characteristics, leading to more innovative solutions.

Crowdfunding: A method of participatory financing, theorised by entrepreneurship experts, in which a large number of people invest small sums in a project or business, enabling entrepreneurs to raise funds without going through traditional investors. The Kickstarter platform has made this collaborative financing model popular.

Crowdsourcing: The practice, described by Jeff Howe, of

outsourcing tasks traditionally carried out in-house to a group of people or to an online community, thereby harnessing collective intelligence and reducing production costs. For example, the Wikipedia website relies on crowdsourcing to create and edit its content.

Innovation life cycle: The successive stages through which an innovation passes, from conception to widespread dissemination and adoption, a concept developed by innovation management researchers. The life cycle model for an innovative product generally includes the phases of exploration, introduction, growth, maturity and decline.

Digital public decision-making: integrating data and digital tools into decision-making.

Design fiction: Creative practice that uses fictional scenarios to imagine potential new products, services or business models. It explores the social, ethical and technological implications of future innovations.

Parametric design: Computer-aided design method that generates shapes from parameters and algorithms. Allows a wide variety of design possibilities to be explored iteratively.

Design for change: Design practice that tackles complex and systemic problems, with a view to fostering positive transformations. Often involves an interdisciplinary approach and close collaboration with stakeholders.

Regenerative design: A design approach that aims to create systems, products and services that restore, regenerate and replenish natural ecosystems. Inspired by the principles of permaculture and the circular economy.

Design sprint: An accelerated design methodology that enables complex problems to be solved in as little as a week. Encourages rapid ideation, rapid prototype testing and agile decision-making.

Design Thinking: A problem-solving method, popularised by IDEO designers, centred on empathy, creativity and rapid iteration, aimed at devising innovative solutions by placing the user at the heart of the design process.

Transdisciplinary design: An approach that transcends traditional disciplinary boundaries to tackle complex problems in a holistic way. Encourages collaboration between experts from different fields to create innovative solutions.

Development on a human scale: An approach proposed by the Chilean economist Manfred Max-Neef, centring development on the fundamental needs and fulfilment of individuals.

Skills development: Concept theorised by experts in training and human resources management, representing the processes by which employees strengthen and acquire new skills.

Cognitive diversity: A concept theorised by innovation researchers, representing the diversity of perspectives, experiences and ways of thinking within a team or group, fostering creativity and innovation. Companies like Google invest in the diversity of their teams to stimulate innovation.

Diversity and inclusion: Concepts theorised by researchers such as Rohini Anand, promoting the value of individual differences (gender, origin, disability, etc.) within companies.

e-Administration (electronic administration) : Digitisation of internal administrative processes and procedures.

Eco-design: integrating environmental considerations into product design.

Sustainable e-Commerce: E-commerce practices that minimise environmental, economic and social impact.

e-Democracy : Using digital technology to facilitate citizen participation.

Circular economy: Economic model, developed by experts in sustainable development, aimed at reducing, reusing, recycling and recovering resources and waste in order to promote a continuous and sustainable life cycle for products and materials. Patagonia has committed to a circular economy approach by recovering and recycling its old clothing.

Behavioural economics: Behavioural economics analyses the impact of psychological, emotional and social factors on the economic decision-making of individuals. Richard Thaler, a behavioural economist, has highlighted the cognitive biases and heuristics that influence economic choices, calling into question the model of rational economic man. His work has applications in public policy and marketing.

Contribution economy: An economic model, theorised by thinkers such as Jeremy Rifkin, that values the voluntary contributions of individuals (time, knowledge, creativity) within communities. Wikipedia is an emblematic example, based on the collaborative work of its volunteer contributors.

Functional economy: Economic model, developed by experts in the sustainable economy, based on the sale of a usage service rather than on the sale of products, promoting the circular economy. Michelin offers mobility solutions based on subscription rather than tyre sales.

Social and solidarity-based economy: Concept developed by thinkers such as Karl Polanyi and Serge Latouche, emphasising forms of economy based on cooperation, solidarity and the primacy of people over capital.

Ecospirituality: A school of thought that integrates spiritual, ecological and holistic perspectives to rethink our relationship with nature and design more sustainable innovations.

Innovation ecosystem: A network of interdependent players (companies, start-ups, universities, investors, etc.) who interact and collaborate to encourage the emergence and dissemination of innovations.

Ecotourism: A form of tourism focused on discovering and preserving nature and local communities.

Education 5.0: Education 5.0 distinguishes itself from traditional educational models by focusing on the development of 21st century skills. It aims to develop individuals capable of innovating, solving

complex problems and adapting to the rapid changes of our time.
Key features of Education 5.0 :

- Learning based on solving real-life problems and devising innovative solutions.
- Active and collaborative teaching methods that encourage creativity, critical thinking and entrepreneurship.
- Tight integration of digital technologies to facilitate access to information and collaboration.
- Stronger links between education and the productive sector, to better align training with the needs of the labour market.
- Developing cross-disciplinary skills such as communication, decision-making and teamwork.

Education 6.0: Developed by Congolese researcher Pitshou Moleka, education 6.0 goes further than education 5.0 by integrating spiritual, emotional and humanist dimensions into the learning process. It aims to train individuals with a global intelligence, capable of giving meaning to their existence and contributing ethically and responsibly to the transformation of society.
Key features of Education 6.0 :

- Developing learners' emotional and spiritual intelligence.
- Learning rooted in values, ethics and the quest for meaning.
- Holistic teaching methods involving the physical, creative and contemplative dimensions.
- Emphasis on well-being, personal development and social responsibility.
- Close links between education, social innovation and sustainable development.
- Transdisciplinary approach and co-construction of knowledge

with stakeholders.

Effectuation: An entrepreneurial approach, developed by Saras Sarasvathy, based on available means and resources rather than predetermined objectives, which encourages innovation. The do-it-yourself entrepreneur who adapts to opportunities as they arise is the embodiment of this effectuation approach.

e-Government : The use of digital technologies to improve the delivery of public services.

Empowerment: A concept developed by theorists of participative management, referring to the process of empowering employees within companies.

Ecological footprint: Indicator developed by William Rees and Mathis Wackernagel, measuring the pressure exerted by human activities on ecosystems.

Renewable energy: Energy sources derived from natural processes, such as the sun, wind or water, developed to reduce dependence on fossil fuels.

Entreprecheur: This concept, developed by Pitshou Moleka, refers to a person capable of combining the skills and expertise of entrepreneur and researcher, combining entrepreneurial creativity and scientific rigour to develop innovative solutions based on scientific research.

Social entrepreneurship: Entrepreneurial practice aimed at solving social problems, improving collective well-being and creating a positive impact on society, a concept promoted by pioneers such as

Muhammad Yunus and his microfinance model. The social enterprise Grameen Bank is an emblematic example.

e-Participation : Involving citizens in decision-making processes via digital means.

Work/life balance: concept developed by organisational psychology researchers to promote better reconciliation between employees' different spheres of life.

Pay equity: Principle of equal pay between men and women for equal work, theorised by labour law and diversity specialists. Example: Many countries have adopted pay equity legislation, as in France with the professional equality index.

Innovation ethics: Reflection on the ethical issues linked to the development and use of innovations, particularly in terms of social responsibility, fairness, data confidentiality and environmental impact.

Employee experience: a concept theorised by human resources and marketing experts, aimed at improving the employee experience and well-being within the company, in the same way as the customer experience.

User Experience (UX): Discipline, developed by experts in ergonomics and design, aimed at designing digital or physical experiences that are pleasant, intuitive and tailored to users' needs. Apple has established itself as a leader in user experience thanks to the meticulous design of its products.

Scalable: Characteristic of a system or service that can be easily extended, developed or reproduced without loss of performance.

Scalability: The ability of a system, service or solution to adapt and scale up to meet growing demand.

Employee retention: A concept developed by human resources management specialists, representing the strategies put in place by companies to retain their most successful and committed employees.

Fintech: Using technology to innovate in the financial services sector, creating solutions to simplify transactions, optimise wealth management or offer online lending services, a concept driven by entrepreneurs and finance experts.

Futuribles: Term coined by Bertrand de Jouvenel, referring to possible and plausible futures. Example: Work of the International Futuribles Association.

Gamification of learning: Gamification consists of integrating fun elements (points, badges, rankings, etc.) into learning environments in order to stimulate learners' motivation, commitment and active involvement.

Metabolic engineering: Discipline of genetic engineering which involves reprogramming the metabolism of living organisms (bacteria, yeast, algae, etc.) to make them produce new molecules or compounds of interest.

Change management : A strategic approach, theorised by management specialists, aimed at supporting organisational transformations in an effective and sustainable way. Example: At

Michelin, change management is essential to support developments linked to the ecological transition.

Skills management: An approach developed by human resources experts, aimed at identifying, enhancing and developing individual and collective skills within an organisation.

Generation management: Approach theorised by human resources experts, aimed at taking into account the differences and expectations of the different generations present within an organisation.

Talent management: Strategic approach developed by human resources experts, aimed at attracting, retaining, developing and promoting the best talent within an organisation. Example: Microsoft has set up a talent management programme to identify and train its future leaders.

Gestion prévisionnelle des emplois et des compétences (GPEC): A strategic approach, conceptualised by human resources experts, aimed at anticipating changes in jobs and skills within an organisation. Example: A company can set up a GPEC to support the digital transformation of its activities.

Reverse globalisation: the tendency, observed by innovation researchers, to develop innovative solutions in emerging countries and then disseminate them in developed markets. The Grameen Bank microfinance model, originally developed in Bangladesh, is an example of this.

Digital hermeneutics: Digital hermeneutics refers to the use of interpretive methods specific to the human sciences to analyse and understand digital artefacts, data and processes.

The principles of digital hermeneutics include :

- Recognition of the contextual and situated nature of understanding digital phenomena.
- Taking account of the subjective and interpretative dimension in data analysis.
- The iterative and dialogical approach to constructing meaning.
- Reflection on the assumptions and biases induced by digital tools and methodologies.

Examples of applications:

- Analysis of the social and cultural dimension of information technologies.
- Study of how individuals and communities appropriate digital technology.
- An understanding of the ethical and political issues surrounding the use of digital technology.

Time horizons: a concept that takes account of different time scales in foresight, theorised by authors such as Michel Godet.

Augmented humanity: A concept that explores ways of enhancing the physical, cognitive and psychological capacities of human beings using technology. It raises ethical and philosophical questions about the nature of the human being.

Digital humanities: digital humanities is an emerging field that explores the intersection between humanities and social sciences disciplines (history, literature, linguistics, philosophy, etc.) and digital technologies. It refers to the use of digital tools and methods for the

study, analysis and representation of data in the humanities and social sciences. They aim to enrich understanding of these disciplines through the contribution of digital technology.
Applications include large-scale text and corpus analysis (text mining, visualisation); the exploitation of databases and digital archives; and the modelling and simulation of social and historical phenomena.

Incubator: A shared workspace where entrepreneurs can develop their ideas and projects, often benefiting from advice, training and resources to help them grow and develop.

Global Innovation Index (GII) : Composite metric used to measure and compare the innovation performance of countries.

Quantum computing: A new approach to computing that exploits quantum phenomena (superposition, entanglement, etc.) to create computers capable of solving certain problems exponentially faster than conventional systems.

Sociotechnical systems engineering: Discipline which studies the interaction between technical and social components within complex systems, in order to design innovations adapted to their organisational and human environment.

Systems engineering: Innovation approach that focuses on the design and integration of interconnected and interdependent systems of systems, with the aim of achieving overall performance.

Bottom-up innovation : Innovation process initiated by end-users or communities, responding to their specific needs and co-creating relevant and adapted solutions, a concept theorised by experts in open innovation. The Wikipedia model, built on contributions from its users, illustrates this type of bottom-up innovation.

Contemplative innovation: An innovative approach inspired by contemplative practices (meditation, mindfulness, etc.) to encourage creativity, problem-solving and decision-making.

Top-down innovation : An innovation process initiated by an organisation's management or R&D teams, often guided by an innovation strategy, a concept developed by innovation management researchers. Apple's innovation of the iPhone smartphone is an emblematic example of top-down innovation.

Disruptive innovation: Radical innovation that disrupts established markets, traditional business models or existing practices by introducing new, original and often high-performance solutions, a concept theorised by Clayton Christensen. The arrival of Netflix on the video-on-demand market has disrupted the DVD industry.

Ethical innovation: Development of innovative solutions that respect high ethical standards, protect privacy, promote social inclusion and contribute to environmental sustainability, a concept promoted by experts in responsible innovation. Fairphone, for example, designs ethical and sustainable smartphones.

Fractal innovation: Creating innovative solutions using fractal models, characterised by the repetition of a pattern at different scales, to design complex, adaptive systems, a concept explored by biomimicry researchers. Biomorphic architecture is inspired by these fractal structures.

Frugal innovation: Designing simple, inexpensive and accessible products or services to meet the needs of low-income populations, by developing affordable, sustainable and effective solutions with limited resources. The Tata Nano, a very low-cost car designed in India, embodies this frugal innovation approach.

Holistic innovation: Adopting a global approach to innovation, integrating social, economic, environmental and cultural dimensions into the process of designing and implementing innovative solutions, a concept developed by sustainable innovation thinkers. Smart and sustainable city initiatives are part of this holistic innovation approach.

Inclusive innovation: Designing innovative solutions that take into account the needs and perspectives of all people, including marginalised or under-represented groups such as indigenous peoples and people living with disabilities.

Incremental Innovation: Gradual and continuous improvement of an existing product, service or process, by making incremental changes, adjustments or additions to increase the value, effectiveness or relevance of the initial innovation, a concept developed by innovation management researchers. Successive smartphone updates illustrate this type of incremental innovation.

Meta-cognitive innovation: The ability of individuals and organisations to reflect critically on their own innovation process, to learn from their successes and failures, and to adapt accordingly in order to progress. This concept has been explored by experts in organisational learning. Innovative companies like 3M encourage this meta-cognitive posture among their employees.

Neural innovation: Design of innovation processes inspired by the functioning of the human brain to encourage connection, creativity, continuous learning and adaptability in the face of rapid changes in the environment, a concept developed by researchers in neuroscience and cognitive science. Design thinking methods are based on this neural innovation approach.

Open innovation : Concept developed by Henry Chesbrough, representing a strategic approach aimed at integrating ideas, technologies and skills from outside the organisation into the innovation process. For example, Procter & Gamble has adopted an open innovation strategy by establishing partnerships with start-ups and universities to accelerate the development of new products. This model combines internal resources with external innovations to increase the company's capacity for innovation.

Quantum innovation: This concept, explored by quantum physics researchers, explores the potential applications of quantum physics in the field of innovation, such as securing communications or developing revolutionary new materials. For example, start-ups such as IQM are working on the design of quantum computers capable of solving complex problems much faster and more efficiently than today's supercomputers. Quantum innovation paves the way for disruptive innovations in many fields.

Social innovation: A concept popularised by thinkers such as Muhammad Yunus, these innovative solutions aim to solve social problems, improve collective well-being and promote inclusion. For example, the Grameen Bank has developed an innovative microfinance model that gives the poorest people in Bangladesh access to credit, thereby contributing to their economic empowerment. Social innovation is characterised by its public-interest purpose and its objective of having a positive impact on society.

Xenosophical innovation: This concept, developed by the innovationologist Pitshou Moleka, encourages us to be open to ideas and perspectives outside our own cultural frame of reference, in order to feed our creativity, broaden our vision and stimulate innovation through the diversity of ideas. For example, companies that draw inspiration from innovative practices from different cultures, such as Japanese discussion circles or African sharing communities, can develop more original solutions that are adapted to the diversity of their global markets.

Innovationology: the emerging science developed through the work of researcher Pitshou Moleka, studying in depth the processes, practices, theories and concepts related to innovation in all its forms.

Artificial intelligence: A field of computer science, theorised by pioneers such as Alan Turing, which studies and develops systems capable of performing tasks that normally require human intelligence, such as voice recognition or trend prediction. For example, virtual assistants such as Siri or Alexa rely on artificial intelligence to interact naturally with users by understanding their language and providing appropriate responses. AI makes it possible to automate and optimise many innovative processes.

Generative artificial intelligence: AI capable of autonomously generating new content (text, images, sounds, etc.). Opens up new creative perspectives and innovative content production.

Collective intelligence: A philosophical and theological concept that sees intelligence as an emergent property of interactions and synergies between individuals, communities and complex systems, with implications for innovation.

Intelligence of use: a concept developed by experts in ergonomics and design, emphasising the need to take in-depth account of the needs, uses and experiences of end users in the innovation process. At Apple, for example, design teams spend a great deal of time observing and understanding user behaviour in order to design products that are intuitive and pleasant to use. This user-centred approach means that innovations can be developed that are relevant and adapted to real-life uses.

Emotional intelligence: Emotional intelligence refers to an individual's ability to understand, manage and use emotions constructively. It encompasses self-awareness, emotion regulation, motivation, empathy and social skills. Characteristics of emotional intelligence :

- Self-awareness: Knowing your own emotions, strengths and weaknesses.

- Self-regulation: The ability to control and channel emotions appropriately.
- Motivation: The inner energy that drives us to action and to fulfilment.
- Empathy: The ability to understand and feel the emotions of others.
- Social skills: The ability to establish and maintain positive, constructive relationships.

Spiritual intelligence or spiritual quotient: Spiritual intelligence refers to an individual's ability to give meaning and depth to his or her existence, to transcend the material to access wider and higher dimensions of reality. It is characterised by a quest for meaning, an inner connection, a heightened awareness and a wisdom that guides action. Key elements of spiritual intelligence :

- Quest for meaning: The search for purpose, meaning and vocation in existence.
- Transcendence: The ability to rise beyond the limited self towards wider and deeper realities.
- Inner connection: A deep link with your own source of inspiration and inner wisdom. - Discernment: The ability to perceive truth and essential reality beyond appearances.
- Wisdom: In-depth knowledge and an enlightened understanding of things.
- Integrity: The alignment between values, thoughts and actions.
- Unity: The recognition of the interdependence and connection of all things.

Territorial intelligence: Mobilising data and networks for local development.

Brain-computer interfaces: Systems enabling direct communication between the human brain and electronic devices. They offer new possibilities for interaction, control and enhancement of human capabilities.

Innovation inputs: Resources and conditions favourable to innovation (institutions, human capital, etc.).

Intrapreneurship: The practice of supporting the entrepreneurial spirit within a company by enabling employees to develop and implement innovative projects. For example, 3M's intrapreneurship programme has enabled employees to create new activities that have generated billions of dollars in sales for the company. This approach fosters internal entrepreneurship and a culture of innovation within organisations.

Reverse intrapreneurship: Concept describing the process by which innovations developed by employees are adopted and promoted by the company's management. For example, the 3M post-it note was first invented by an employee before being supported and marketed on a large scale by management. This model of inverted intrapreneurship makes it possible to value the initiative and creativity of employees within the organisation.

Digital twins: Virtual models of objects, processes or systems that faithfully reflect their physical counterparts.
Simulate, optimise and anticipate the performance of real systems.

Agile leadership: The leader adapts quickly to change and encourages experimentation and continuous learning of new methods and approaches.

Ambidextrous leadership: Ambidextrous leadership refers to the leader's ability to manage exploitation (optimising existing activities) and exploration (seeking out new opportunities) in a balanced way. It is a form of innovation in leadership because it requires :

- Bringing together and coordinating two sometimes conflicting approaches: efficiency and innovation
- Adapt your leadership style to the needs of the moment, moving

from a controlling to a facilitating role

- Creating an organisational culture that encourages ambidexterity, with spaces dedicated to experimentation. Examples of companies that have adopted this type of leadership: 3M, Google, Amazon.

Collaborative leadership: The leader facilitates collaboration between team members to achieve common goals.

Conscious leadership: Conscious leadership involves awareness of oneself, others and the context. The conscious leader shows empathy and compassion and seeks to encourage the development of his or her colleagues.

Holistic leadership: Holistic leadership adopts a 360-degree vision, taking into account the overall well-being of employees (physical, mental, emotional, spiritual). The holistic leader seeks to develop everyone's potential in a balanced way.

Shared leadership: Rather than a single leader, leadership is distributed within a team, enabling collective decision-making.

Living Lab: Open, participative innovation spaces that enable businesses, universities, public institutions and citizens to work together to test, experiment and co-create new solutions and services. For example, the Living Lab of the city of Malmo in Sweden involves local residents in the development of innovative urban projects such as sustainable mobility systems and eco-friendly housing. These facilities encourage bottom-up innovation and user involvement.

Community living lab: A variation on the living lab concept, these

innovation spaces are anchored in a local community, enabling citizens to co-design innovative solutions that meet their specific needs. For example, the Living Lab of the city of Grenoble in France brings residents together to devise innovations that improve the quality of life in their neighbourhoods, such as shared gardening systems or inclusive mobility services.
This bottom-up approach harnesses the collective intelligence of a community.

Digital literacy: Digital literacy refers to the set of skills needed to use information and communication technologies effectively, critically and ethically. It goes beyond simply mastering digital tools.

Speculative literature: Literary genre exploring the imaginary consequences of technological, social or environmental change, stimulating reflection on possible futures.

Experiential marketing: A strategy aimed at creating memorable and engaging experiences for consumers.

Viral marketing: A marketing strategy that seeks to exploit social networks to amplify the spread of a message.

Smart materials : Materials with "intelligent" properties that enable them to adapt dynamically to their environment or to external stimuli (temperature, pressure, electric field, etc.), opening the way to innovative applications.

Regenerative medicine: field of medicine aimed at restoring, maintaining or improving the functions of damaged or deficient tissues and organs, using stem cells, tissue engineering or gene therapies.

Metaverse: Concept of an interconnected and persistent virtual universe, accessible via different devices. Paves the way for new forms of immersive, social and economic experiences.

Microfinance: Developed by pioneers such as Muhammad Yunus and the Grameen Bank, microfinance aims to provide financial services to people excluded from the traditional banking system. Example: Bank Rakyat's microcredit programme in Indonesia.

Scaling up: The process of expanding and deploying a successful small-scale innovation on a larger scale.

Circular business model: A concept developed by circular economy experts, this economic model aims to completely rethink the design, production, use and end-of-life processes of products and services to minimise waste and environmental impacts.

Patagonia, for example, has adopted a circular business model, offering its customers the opportunity to repair, reuse or recycle their used clothing. This model helps to extend the life cycle of products.

Collaborative business model: A concept theorised by experts in open innovation, this economic model is based on a logic of collaboration between different stakeholders (companies, users, suppliers, etc.) to co-create and share value.

Concentrator business model: A concept developed by strategy experts, this business model consists of positioning oneself as a "concentrator" that brings together, connects and puts in contact different players within an ecosystem. For example, the Amazon platform has established itself as a hub by bringing together a large number of sellers, suppliers and customers on its platform, taking advantage of network effects.

Long tail business model: Theorised by Chris Anderson, this business model aims to take advantage of the variety and low demand of niche products, complementing the products that account for the majority of sales. For example, the online bookshop Amazon has been able to develop this long tail model by offering a wide choice of books, including titles that are not widely sold, thus complementing the bestsellers.

Servitisation business model: A concept developed by experts in the functional economy, this business model involves selling the use of a product rather than the product itself, by offering services and solutions tailored to customers' needs. For example, Michelin sells tyre mobility and maintenance contracts rather than tyres, thereby promoting a logic of use rather than ownership.

Frugal business model: A concept theorised by experts in inclusive innovation, this business model aims to design affordable, simple and sustainable products and services, using limited resources, to meet the needs of low-income populations. For example, the Indian company Tata developed the Tata Nano, a very low-cost car, by adopting a frugal innovation approach.

Multi-sided business model: Theorised by economists, this business model consists of linking different groups of users by subsidising access to one group in order to generate value with the other. For example, social networking platforms such as Facebook offer their services to users free of charge, while monetising the relationship with advertisers.

Use-oriented business model: A concept developed by experts in the functional economy, this business model focuses on selling the use of a product rather than selling it directly. For example, Rolls-Royce sells flight hours rather than aircraft engines, providing maintenance and after-sales service.

Platform business model: A concept theorised by strategy experts, this business model involves creating a platform that facilitates interactions and exchanges between different groups of users. For example, Airbnb has developed a digital platform that brings hosts and travellers together, generating value through commission on bookings.

Reverse innovation business model: A concept developed by experts in innovation management, this business model involves designing innovative products or services in emerging countries, then distributing them in developed markets.

For example, car manufacturer Renault first developed the Logan, an affordable car designed for Indian consumers, before successfully exporting it to Europe.

Servitised business model: A variant of the servitisation model, this business model aims to sell services and solutions tailored to customer needs rather than products. For example, Xerox has developed a photocopier rental model that includes maintenance, document management and consultancy services, rather than focusing solely on the sale of equipment.

Triple win business model: A concept developed by experts in social innovation, this business model aims to create value for three stakeholders: customers, the company and society. For example, the social enterprise Grameen Danone has developed a low-cost, nutritious yoghurt for poor populations, while generating profits for the company and improving local food security.

Multi-agent modelling and simulation: Computer modelling techniques that simulate complex interactions between multiple autonomous agents (individuals, organisations, robots, etc.), to test and design innovations in virtual environments.

Neurophilosophy: Neurophilosophy studies the links between the functioning of the brain and philosophical issues such as consciousness, morality and decision-making. Neurophilosopher Patricia Churchland shows how discoveries in neuroscience are challenging certain traditional philosophical assumptions and opening up new perspectives on the nature of the human mind.

New economy: Term used to describe the profound structural changes in the economy, characterised by the growing importance of digital technology, innovation, the knowledge economy and services. The rise of digital platforms, the collaborative economy and artificial intelligence illustrate this transition to a new economy.

Programmed obsolescence: The practice of intentionally limiting a product's lifespan in order to encourage faster replacement, a concept studied by experts in the circular economy. This practice is being challenged by movements in favour of extending the life of products and the circular economy.

Objective-compatibility: The ability of an innovation to align with and contribute to the achievement of broader strategic, social, environmental or political objectives, a concept developed by innovation management experts. For example, green innovations that reduce the environmental footprint are said to be "objective-compatible" with sustainable development issues.

Onboarding: Process of integrating and supporting new employees, conceptualised by human resources specialists, to make it easier for them to take up their position and adapt to the company.

Open data: A concept promoted by experts in open innovation, referring to free and open access to public or private data, enabling it to be re-used to create new applications and innovative services. For example, many cities have adopted open data policies to share data on mobility, the environment and town planning.

Citizen participation: Approach aimed at actively involving citizens in decision-making processes, theorised by authors such as Jürgen Habermas.

Design Thinking: A problem-solving method, popularised by IDEO designers, centred on empathy, creativity and rapid iteration, aimed at designing innovative solutions by placing the user at the heart of the design process. For example, the design of the Roomba robot hoover was based on a design thinking approach to understand user needs and develop a product that is intuitive and pleasant to use.

Systems thinking: An approach developed by theorists such as Edgar Morin, aimed at understanding the complexity of phenomena in a holistic way.

Design philosophy: A field of thought that examines the philosophical, ethical and existential dimensions underlying the design and innovation processes.

Pitch: A pitch is a concise and persuasive presentation of an idea, project or company, designed to arouse the interest and commitment of a target audience (investors, partners, customers, etc.).

Open innovation platform: Concept developed by open innovation experts, representing a digital or physical space that facilitates collaboration, idea sharing and co-creation between different players (companies, start-ups, academics, users, etc.).

Multi-faceted platform: A concept developed by economists to describe a business model that connects two or more interdependent user groups by subsidising access to one group in order to generate value with the other. For example, social networks such as Facebook offer their service free of charge to end users, while monetising the relationship with advertisers.

Global positioning: Rank and relative position of a country in the GII rankings.

Proof of Concept (POC): A crucial stage in the innovation process, where a new idea, technology or solution is tested and validated on a small scale to prove its feasibility and potential before moving on to a larger development phase. This POC phase helps to reduce risk and refine the concept before wider deployment.

Organisational proactivity: An organisation's ability to anticipate change, identify new opportunities and adapt early, thereby fostering agility and innovation. Proactive companies like 3M encourage their teams to question existing practices and explore new avenues.

Agile innovation process: A flexible, iterative approach to developing innovations, characterised by short design, test and continuous improvement cycles, a concept popularised by agile methods in IT. This agility makes it possible to adapt more quickly to user feedback and market developments.

Genetic programming: An artificial intelligence technique inspired by the mechanisms of biological evolution, in which algorithms automatically generate computer programmes or innovative solutions through an iterative process of selection, crossover and mutation. This approach allows unexpected innovations to emerge.

Strategic foresight: a discipline developed by management experts, aimed at anticipating and preparing for future changes in the environment, technologies and markets, in order to guide strategic decisions and innovation within the company. This forward-looking thinking helps to imagine new business models and seize emerging opportunities.

Territorial foresight: An approach to foresight applied to local and regional scales, theorised by authors such as Hugues de Jouvenel. Example: Foresight approach of the Grand Est region in France.

Rapid prototyping: A practice derived from design thinking, involving the rapid design and testing of simplified versions of a product or service to obtain feedback from users and iterate on the concept. This agile approach speeds up the innovation process by iteratively validating hypotheses.

Augmented reality: Technology that enhances the perception of the real world by integrating virtual elements. It offers new possibilities for interaction and innovative experiences.

Extended reality: An approach encompassing augmented reality, virtual reality and their combinations. Enables immersive, fluid experiences to be created between the physical and digital worlds.

Recognition at work: Concept developed by experts in employee motivation and commitment, representing the importance of valuing employees' contributions and achievements.

Resilience: The ability of a system to absorb change and reorganise itself while retaining its functions and structure, a concept developed by researchers such as C.S. Holling.

Organisational resilience: A concept developed by management researchers, representing an organisation's ability to bounce back and adapt to situations of crisis or change. Example
The COVID-19 pandemic highlighted the importance of organisational resilience for many companies.

Problem solving by analogy: An innovation technique that involves drawing inspiration from existing solutions in other fields to solve a specific problem, a concept developed by creativity researchers. For example, Michelin tyre designers were inspired by the structure of animal paw prints to design treads with better grip.

Dissociative problem solving: An innovation method that involves questioning logical links and habitual associations of ideas, in order to imagine new perspectives and solutions, a concept theorised by creativity experts. This approach allows you to think outside the box and generate unexpected innovations.

Incubative problem solving: An innovation technique based on activating the unconscious process of the mind, by letting the problem "incubate" for a certain period of time before returning to conscious thought, a concept developed by researchers in cognitive psychology. This method encourages the emergence of creative and original ideas.

Morphological problem solving: A systematic method of innovation that involves breaking down a complex problem into sub-problems, then recombining these elements in original ways to generate new solutions, a concept theorised by creativity experts. This structured approach stimulates divergent thinking.

Reframing problem solving: An innovation technique that involves reformulating a problem in such a way as to open up new perspectives and possibilities for solutions, by adopting a different frame of reference, a concept developed by creativity researchers. For example, reframing a "food waste" problem as a "circular economy" opportunity can stimulate more sustainable innovations.

Problem solving by questioning: An innovation method that encourages people to question existing assumptions, beliefs and paradigms in order to come up with new and disruptive solutions, a concept theorised by creativity experts. This approach challenges established mental models to stimulate divergent thinking.

Synectic problem solving: An innovation technique that uses analogy and metaphor to make unexpected connections and generate new ideas, a concept developed by creativity researchers. This method encourages lateral thinking and the association of apparently distant elements to stimulate innovation.

Corporate Social Responsibility (CSR): Concept theorised by management researchers, representing the voluntary commitment of companies to take account of social, environmental and ethical issues in their activities.

360-degree feedback: Gather feedback from employees, peers and superiors to improve self-assessment.

Retrofit: Concept developed by experts in the circular economy, referring to the fact of modernising, updating or transforming an existing product to give it a new life, rather than replacing it. For example, retrofitting internal combustion vehicles into electric vehicles extends the life of cars while making them more environmentally friendly.

Industrial Revolution 4.0: A concept describing the profound transformation of production systems, theorised by strategy and management experts and characterised by the integration of digital technologies, artificial intelligence, the Internet of Things and robotics into industrial processes. This new industrial revolution is overturning business models and innovation practices.

Technology roadmap: A strategic planning tool developed by innovation management experts, designed to anticipate future technological developments and identify medium- and long-term innovation opportunities. This mapping of technological trajectories helps organisations to direct their innovation efforts in a coherent way.

Regulatory sandbox: An emerging concept, inspired by computer "sandboxes", referring to an experimental and flexible regulatory framework enabling innovative companies to test new products, services or business models in a controlled manner, without having to comply immediately with all the regulations in force. This approach aims to encourage innovation by reducing regulatory barriers.

Future scenarios: A method of exploring alternative futures, used by futurists such as Pierre Wack. Example: 2050 scenarios for the EUFORIE project in Europe.

Schumpeter theory: Theory developed by the economist Joseph Schumpeter, according to which innovation is the main driving force behind economic development, through creative destruction, i.e. the replacement of old economic models by new, more efficient ones. This vision of innovation as a process of permanent renewal has strongly influenced thinking on entrepreneurship and business competitiveness.

Weak signals: Concept developed by the sociologist Igor Ansoff, referring to early indications of potential changes in the environment.

Sociology of innovation: Study of the interactions between technological, economic or organisational innovations and the social, cultural and political dynamics that shape them.

Food sovereignty: Concept promoted by farmers' movements such as La Via Campesina, defining the right of peoples to decide on their own food and farming systems. Example: Food sovereignty initiatives in West Africa.

Blue ocean strategy: Concept theorised by strategy researchers Kim and Mauborgne, designating a value innovation approach aimed at creating new, uncontested market spaces, rather than facing intense competition in existing markets (the "red oceans"). This approach makes it possible to free oneself from competition and concentrate on creating value for customers.

Niche strategy: A concept developed by strategy experts to describe an approach to innovation that involves positioning oneself in a narrow, specialised market segment, rather than targeting a mass market. This strategy makes it possible to stand out from the competition and respond more effectively to the specific needs of a group of customers.

National innovation system: A concept developed by economists to designate all the institutions, companies, universities and public policies that interact to promote innovation in a country or region. Analysing and strengthening these innovation systems is a strategic challenge for many countries.

Disruptive technology: A concept theorised by Clayton Christensen, referring to a technological innovation that disrupts an existing market by introducing radically different and more efficient products or services, rendering existing technologies obsolete. For example, the arrival of the portable digital music player greatly disrupted the compact disc industry.

Emerging technology : Concept describing a new technology under development, whose applications and potential impact on society and the economy are not yet fully known or mastered. For example, blockchain, artificial intelligence and biotechnology are considered to be emerging technologies, whose potential for innovation is still being explored.

Frugal technology: A concept developed by experts in inclusive innovation, referring to the development of simple, affordable and robust technologies that meet the essential needs of low-income populations, by adapting to local resource and infrastructure constraints. For example, low-cost medical devices designed for developing countries are part of this frugal technology approach.

Pervasive technology: A concept describing technologies that are ubiquitous and integrated into our everyday environment, such as the Internet of Things, augmented reality and ambient intelligence. These 'penetrating' technologies are profoundly transforming the way we use and interact with the world around us, paving the way for new innovations.

Green technology: a set of technologies, products and services designed to reduce environmental impact, a concept promoted by specialists such as Paul Hawken.

Vertiginous technology: Concept referring to radical technological innovations with potentially massive and unpredictable impacts on society, the economy and the environment. For example, the development of general artificial intelligence, capable of equalling or surpassing human intelligence, is considered a vertiginous technology because of its uncertain societal consequences.

Teleworking: Remote working method, conceptualised by

management experts, enabling employees to carry out their work away from company premises. Example: The COVID-19 pandemic accelerated the widespread adoption of teleworking in many organisations.

Theology of innovation: Theological approach that explores the spiritual, moral and symbolic dimensions of technological, social and cultural innovations, particularly their implications for the transformation of human beings and their existence.

Sustainable tourism: A tourism approach that minimises environmental and socio-cultural impact, while generating local economic benefits.

Regenerative tourism: Tourism that aims to restore, revitalise and regenerate the natural and social systems of destinations.

Digital transformation: Adopting new technologies to improve agility and collaboration.

Transhumanism: Intellectual and cultural movement that advocates the use of technology to improve the physical and cognitive capacities of human beings, paving the way for controversial biomedical innovations.

Transition: Process of long-term transformation of socio-technical systems, theorised by researchers such as Franck Geels.
Example: Energy transition with the gradual phase-out of nuclear power.

Shared value : Concept developed by Michael Porter and Mark Kramer, describing an approach to innovation that aims to create economic value while generating social and environmental benefits. This approach is based on the identification of intersections between the interests of the company and the needs of society, enabling the development of mutually beneficial solutions.

Strategic intelligence: Systematic process of observing and analysing the external environment (competitive, technological, regulatory, etc.) to identify weak signals, emerging trends and innovation opportunities at an early stage. This concept has been developed by experts in innovation management. This intelligence feeds into strategic thinking and guides innovation efforts.

Zero waste: A concept promoted by citizens' movements and experts in the circular economy, aimed at rethinking production and consumption patterns to eliminate waste completely, taking inspiration from natural cycles.
This holistic approach to sustainable innovation guides many eco-design, reuse and recycling initiatives.

Zone of proximal learning: Concept developed by the psychologist Lev Vygotski, referring to the gap between what an individual can achieve on their own and what they can achieve with the help of a more experienced person. This zone of potential development is crucial for stimulating innovation, by placing individuals or teams in challenging situations that are slightly superior to their current skills.

Innovation zone: Concept designating a delimited geographical area, public or private, which brings together a concentration of innovative companies, research centres, incubators and infrastructures that encourage collaboration and the emergence of new initiatives. For example, competitiveness clusters, technopoles and innovation districts are areas that are conducive to innovation.

Innovation free zone: An emerging concept, designating a defined area benefiting from a specific regulatory and tax framework, aimed at attracting and facilitating the establishment of innovative companies. These free zones generally offer advantages in terms of taxation, intellectual property or access to talent, with the aim of stimulating innovation and entrepreneurship.

Zoom in / zoom out: Innovation techniques derived from design thinking, involving alternating between a "zoom in" approach, focusing on details and the user experience, and a "zoom out" approach, focusing on the overall vision and strategic issues. This back-and-forth approach helps to refine innovations while aligning them with the wider objectives of the organisation.

SELECTED BIBLIOGRAPHY

1. Christensen, C. M. (2015). Disruptive innovation. Pearson.

2. Geels, F. W. (2004). From the coexistence of socio-technical regimes to system transitions. Cahiers du CERC, (1), 5568.

3. Habermas, J. (1997). Law and Democracy: Between Facts and Norms. Gallimard.

4. Hawken, P. (2011). The ecology of commerce: a manifesto for a sustainable economy. Éditions d'Organisation.

5. de Jouvenel, B. (1964). L'art de la conjecture. Éditions du Rocher.

6. Kim, W. C., & Mauborgne, R. (2010). Blue Ocean Strategy. Pearson.

7. Moleka, P. (2024). Innovationology: Exploring an Emerging Science. Tome 1.

8. Moleka, P. (2024). Innovationology: Exploring an Emerging Science. Tome 2.

9. Moleka. P. (2024). Holistic Transformation of the Democratic Republic of Congo: Innovative Model and Roadmap for Sustainable and Multidimensional Prosperity.

10. Porter, M. E., & Kramer, M. R. (2011). Creating Shared Value. Harvard Business Review, 89(1/2), 62-77.

11. Sarasvathy, S. D. (2005). What Makes Entrepreneurs

Entrepreneurial? Darden Business Publishing.

12. Thaler, R. H., & Sunstein, C. R. (2010). Nudge. The gentle way to inspire the right decision. Vuibert.

13. Rees, W. E., & Wackernagel, M. (1999). Our ecological footprint. Écosociété.

14. Yunus, M. (2007). Towards a world without poverty. JC Lattès.

MIX
Papier aus verantwortungsvollen Quellen
Paper from responsible sources
FSC® C105338

Printed by Books on Demand GmbH, Norderstedt / Germany